········ CARLOS ACOSTA ········

# TOCORORO

## A CUBAN TALE

### PHOTOGRAPHS BY ANGELA TAYLOR

for Jane King

OBERON BOOKS
LONDON

Published in 2004 by Oberon Books Ltd

Oberon Books (incorporating Absolute Classics)
521 Caledonian Road, London N7 9RH
Tel: 020 7607  Fax: 020 7607 3629
oberon.books@btinternet.com
www.oberonbooks.com

ISBN: 1 84002 488 7

Cover and book design: Jeff Willis

Printed in Great Britain by G&B Printers, Hanworth, Middlesex

## Introduction (English)

For a long time I had an idea that wouldn't let me sleep. It haunted me in the evenings, at night, during rehearsals and performances; everywhere: New York, London, Budapest, Havana… Could I tell a story through dance as others have done before? I couldn't think about anything else. My instinct and my subconscious fought a constant battle. While one encouraged me: Of course you can! The other dissuaded me, saying: But, have you gone mad, have you thought about the consequences? With all this uncertainty I found it hard to concentrate on my ballet. These voices appeared at all hours in my head. One day I said: enough! And on a beautiful Havana evening, sitting at home on the terrace, I wrote a story inspired by my own life: *Tocororo: a Cuban tale*.

I talked to Sadler's Wells. 'You need a producer. I think Andy Wood is the man for you', suggested Alistair Spalding. Right away, Sharon Ray introduced me to Salvatore Forino for the designs. Once some of the early images of what the show would be like were created, I showed them to Andy. After several meetings and talks he made up his mind: 'I like the idea. Let's do it.'

Having worked out the budget it was time to look for sponsors. The UCLA for The Performing Arts in Los Angeles seemed keen. We got together in New York. I explained what the show was about the best I could. There was lots of excitement and lots of interest, yet when the project was about to take off, the eleventh of September catastrophe occurred and everything fell through. London beckoned us. Andy talked to several theatres until he finally managed to get a deal with Sadler's Wells. Everything was now ready to start; we had the theatre, the dates, the designs and the funding: our only difficulty now was putting together a show. It was then that I became nervous. I had to create a show, but how could someone who had never before choreographed come up with something of such scope? How was I going to bring to life so many ideas in my head? The voices in my subconscious started again: I told you plainly you had gone crazy! I ended up doing what I've always done: listening to my instincts. Two years after that Havana twilight, with the collaboration of an excellent team and brilliant dancers, at last our baby opened its eyes to life.

Here it is. Enjoy it!

Translator: Ruswel Piñeiro

## Presentación (Spanish)

La interrogante desde hacía mucho tiempo merodeaba por los rincones de mi cabeza y no me dejaba dormir. Me perseguía en las tardes, las noches, durante ensayos y funciones; por cualquier parte: New York, Londres, Budapest, La Habana… ¿Podría yo en la danza contar una historia como lo han hecho otros? No atinaba a pensar en otra cosa. Así, casi sin darme aviso, comenzaron a batallar mi instinto y mi subconsciente. Uno me alentaba: ¡Claro que puedes!, y el otro lo callaba diciendo: ¿Pero, te has vuelto loco, has pensado en las consecuencias? En esta incertidumbre permanecí, al extremo que me costaba concentrarme en el ballet. Aquellas voces surgían a toda hora en mi cabeza. Un día dije: ¡basta! Y una tarde hermosamente habanera, en la terraza de mi casa, escribí una historia inspirándome en la mía personal: *Tocororo: a Cuban tale*.

Hablé con el Sadler's Wells. 'You need a producer. I think Andy Wood is the man for you' fue la propuesta de Alistair Spalding. Enseguida, Sharon Ray me presentó a Salvatore Forino para los diseños y, una vez confeccionadas algunas imágenes primitivas de lo que sería el espectáculo, se las mostré a Andy. Después de varias reuniones y debates, Andy se decidió: 'I like the idea. Let's do it.'

Hecho el presupuesto, se imponía pensar en quién lo iba a auspiciar. El UCLA for The Performing Arts en Los Ángeles parecía interesado, junto con otras avenidas. Nos reunimos en New York. Expliqué lo mejor que pude el espectáculo. Muchas emociones, mucho interés; mas a punto de despegar el proyecto vino la catástrofe del once de septiembre y se jodió todo. Londres nos hacía guiños. Andy entabló diálogos con distintos teatros hasta que al final consiguió llegar a un acuerdo con el Sadler's Wells. Ya todo estaba listo para arrancar: teatro, fechas, diseños y financiamiento: sólo faltaba el show. Entonces, fue cuando me entró el nerviosismo. Tenía que crear un espectáculo y, ¿cómo podría alguien, que en su vida nunca había coreografiado, producir algo de esta magnitud?, ¿de qué manera iba a materializar tantas ideas forjadas en mi cabeza? Comenzaron nuevamente las voces de mi subconsciente: ¡Te lo dije bien claro que te habías vuelto loco! Terminé haciendo lo de siempre: escuchar a mi instinto. Dos años después de aquel crepúsculo habanero, con la colaboración de un excelente equipo de trabajo y de valiosos bailarines y bailarinas, ¡por fin! abrió sus ojos a la vida nuestro bebé.

Aquí está. ¡Disfrútenlo!

# CUBA
## Countryside and City

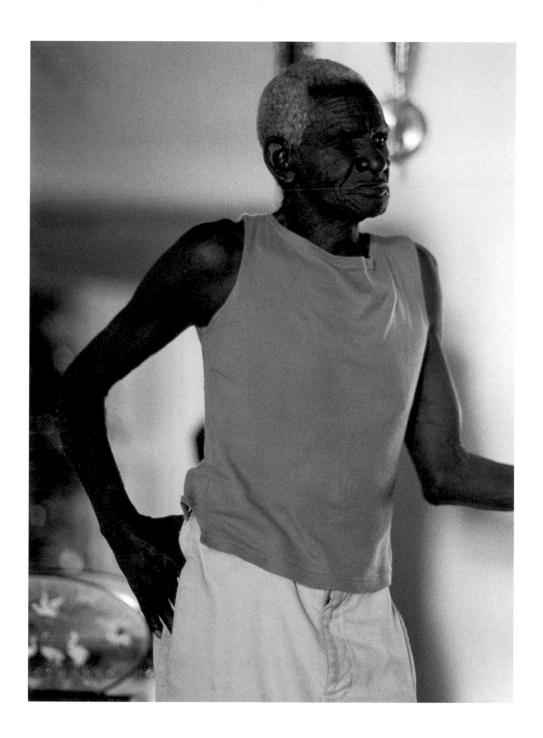

Pedro Acosta, Carlos' father

# Rehearsing at the García Lorca Theatre

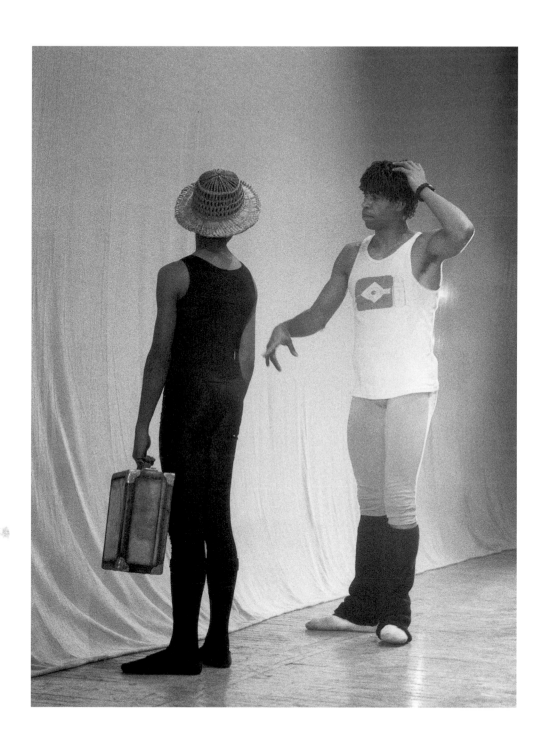

## TOCCORORO: A CUBAN TALE
## in Performance

Tocororo is a boy from the Cuban countryside. His father persuades him to go to the city in search of new possibilities. Once there, Tocororo faces many difficulties that lead him to question his decision to stay. He learns what love is but when his happiness is almost complete he finds he must choose the direction his life will take. How important are his aspirations? What will his dreams cost him?

These and other questions are posed in this dazzling spectacle inspired by Cuba, its dances, music and rhythms.

Tocororo es un niño cubano del campo. Su padre lo convence para que vaya a la ciudad en busca de una vida mejor. Allí, Tocororo se enfrenta a muchas dificultades que lo hacen reflexionar sobre si se queda o no. Aprende lo que significa amar, pero cuando su felicidad es casi completa debe decidir qué rumbo tomará su vida. ¿Cuán importante son sus aspiraciones? ¿Cuánto le costarán sus sueños? Éstas y otras preguntas aparecen representadas en este espectáculo deslumbrante inspirado en Cuba, sus danzas, su música y sus ritmos.

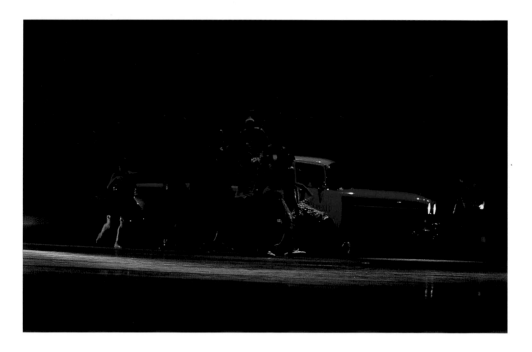

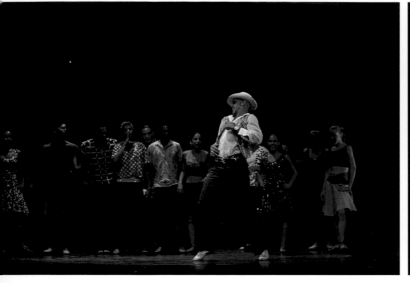

**First Pas de deux**

**Father's death**

**Moor and ladies**

**Dominoes game**

**Clarita's Solo**

Fidel Castro

Carlos and his mother, Maria Quesada

CAST

Tocororo: Carlos Acosta
Tocororo (as a boy): Yonah Acosta
Father: Michel Ávalos
Clarita: Verónica Corveas
The Santera (Havana): Hilda Oates
The Santera (London): Mireya Chapman
The Moor: Alexander Varona
Townspeople: Soloists and corps de ballet from
DANZA CONTEMPORÁNEA DE CUBA
Diane Cabrera/Jessie Gutierrez/Alena León
Yaday Ponce/Odeymis Torres/Nadiezhda Valdés
Michel Ávalos/George Céspedes/Wuislley Estacholi
Miguel Hunaga/Julio César Iglesias/Alain Rivero

MUSICIANS

José Varona (bass)
Hammadi Recurrell (percussion)
Yadasny Portillo (Keyboards)
Dreiser Durruthy (batá)
Dismer Hechavarría (tumbadora)

Choreography and Libretto: Carlos Acosta
Design: Salvatore Forino
Music: Miguel Núñez
Lighting: Carlos Repilado
Assistants to the choreographer: Gladys Acosta
and René De Cárdenas

Tocororo was premiered at Gran Teatro de la Habana Sala
'García Lorca' on February 15th, 2003 and received its London
premiere at Sadler's Wells Theatre July 15th 2003

Director General: Carlos Acosta
Executive Producer: Andy Wood for Como No
Company Manager: Heriberto Cabezas
Production Manager: Antonio Linares
Stage Manager: Luis Carlos Benvenuto
Wardrobe: Marilín Acosta

ACKNOWLEDGEMENTS
Thanks to: Alicia Alonso; The Cuban National Ballet; Miguel Iglesias;
Alberto Díaz; The Cuban National Council for Dramatic Arts,
Ramona de Sáa; The Cuban National Ballet School, Gayle Miller
and Malcolm Grant, Capezio.

CARLOS ACOSTA, Principal Guest Artist with The Royal Ballet, was born in Cuba in 1973. He started dancing at the insistence of his father as a means of occupying his spare time. He began dancing at the National Ballet School of Cuba, Havana, when he was ten. In June 1991 he received his diploma with maximum qualifications and a gold medal.

He has won numerous awards ranging from the Gold Medal at the Prix de Lausanne (January 1990), Grand Prix and Gold Medal at the Fourth Annual Competition of Ballet in Paris (November 1990), and the Grand Prix in the third Juvenile Competition of Dance (June 1991). His most recent accolade was the International Critics' Prize from the Chilean dance critics.

From 1989 to 1991 he performed throughout the world, guesting with many other companies including ballet companies in Italy, Mexico and Venezuela. In the 1991/92 season he was invited to dance with the English National Ballet in London. He made his debut in the 'Polovtsian Dances' from *Prince Igor* and also appeared as the Prince in Ben Stevenson's *The Nutcracker* and *Cinderella*, partnering Eva Evdokimova and Ludmilla Semenyaka.

From 1992 to 1993 he danced as a member of the National Ballet of Cuba. In October 1993 and September 1994 he toured with the company to Madrid, Spain where he danced the principal roles in *Giselle*, *Don Quixote* and *Swan Lake*.

In November 1993 he was invited to join the Houston Ballet as a principal dancer where he made his American stage debut as the Prince in Stevenson's *The Nutcracker*. Following this his repertory with the Houston Ballet included Prince Siegfried in *Swan Lake*, Solor in the third act of *La Bayadère*, Basilio in *Don Quixote*, Stevenson's *Britten Pas de Deux*, the male lead in Harald Lander's *Etudes*, and Jiri Kylian's *Symphony in D*.

Acosta made his first appearance with The Royal Ballet in William Forsythe's *In the middle, somewhat elevated* in October 1998 and subsequently appeared as Jean de Brienne in Rudolf Nureyev's production of *Raymonda* Act III, Colas in Frederick Ashton's *La Fille mal gardée*, Siegfried in *Swan Lake*, Actaeon in the *Diana & Actaeon* pas de deux. His MacMillan repertory includes The Brother in Kenneth MacMillan's *My Brother, My Sisters*, Solo Boy in *Gloria*, Des Grieux in MacMillan's *Manon*, and the Messenger of Death in *Song of the Earth*. Other roles include Albrecht in Peter Wright's production of *Giselle*, the Principal Boy in *Rhapsody*, Nacho Duato's *Remanso*, The Prince in Peter Wright's production of *The Nutcracker*, Franz in Ninette de Valois' production of *Coppélia*, Nijinsky's *L'Après-midi d'un faune*, the Boy with Matted Hair in Anthony Tudor's *Shadowplay* and Basilio in Nureyev's *Don Quixote*.

*Tocororo* is his first piece as director and choreographer.